COLOUR

CODES

Teresa Heapy

OXFORD
UNIVERSITY PRESS

OXFORD
UNIVERSITY PRESS

Great Clarendon Street, Oxford, OX2 6DP, United Kingdom

Oxford University Press is a department of the University of Oxford. It furthers the University's objective of excellence in research, scholarship, and education by publishing worldwide. Oxford is a registered trade mark of Oxford University Press in the UK and in certain other countries

British Library Cataloguing in Publication Data
Data available

ISBN: 978-0-19-830801-0

10 9 8 7 6 5 4 3 2

Paper used in the production of this book is a natural, recyclable product made from wood grown in sustainable forests. The manufacturing process conforms to the environmental regulations of the country of origin.

Printed in China by Hing Yip

Acknowledgements

Series Editor: Nikki Gamble

Designed and typeset by Ana Cosma

Cover photo by Hintau Aliaksei/Shutterstock

The publishers would like to thank the following for the permission to reproduce photographs: **p1/p18l/23:** Dirk Ercken/Alamy; **p2/3:** Moophoto/Dreamstime.com; **p4:** Getty Images/Barcroft Media; **p4/5:** Switch32/amanaimagesRF/Getty Images; **p5:** Wayne Lynch/All Canada Photos/Corbis; **p6/22:** Willi Schmitz/Getty Images; **p7/22:** WILDLIFE GmbH/Alamy; **p8b/22:** F1online digitale Bildagentur GmbH/Alamy; **p8t/23:** Evgeniya Moroz/Shutterstock; **p9:** Alcibbum Photography/Corbis; **p10/22:** Carol Yepes/Getty Images; **p11b:** Steve Winter/Getty Images; **p11t/23:** Alaska Stock/Corbis; **p12/23:** Thomas Marent/Minden Pictures/Corbis; **p13/23:** Jasenka Luksa/Shutterstock; **p14l/22:** Gary Bell/OceanwideImages.com; **p14r:** Image ID: 0128420-NMA. Copyright © Nigel Marsh/SeaPics.com; **p15/22:** Beth Swanson/Shutterstock; **p16/23:** Anup Shah/Corbis; **p17:** Alucard2100/Shutterstock; **p18r:** Adam Jones/Visuals Unlimited/Corbis; **p19/23:** Getty Images/Mark Kostich; **p20/23:** Gary Bell/OceanwideImages.com; **p24:** MPanchenko/Shutterstock; **back cover:** Gary Bell/OceanwideImages.com

Contents

Colour in Nature

There are so many colours in nature!

Plants and animals use colours for many different reasons. What are they trying to say? Are they hiding? Or are they showing off?

Colours are used to send many different messages.

to hide

Colour codes

Look out for these codes in this book!

To Hide

To Be Seen

to be seen

Food I Eat

! To Warn Off!

To Hunt

Look at Me!

Some plants have very bright colours
so that insects and birds will notice them.

Flowers need bees to carry their **pollen**
to other flowers. They use bright colours
to **attract** the bees.

Most bees like purple and blue flowers best.

pollen

Some plants have bright <u>berries</u>, which contain seeds. Birds eat the berries and fly away. Later, the seeds come out in the birds' poo! This helps new plants to grow in different places.

Some plants grow red berries so birds can find them easily.

berries

I'm the Best!

The male peacock uses his colourful tail to attract a female. He spreads it out like a fan and shakes it!

eyespot

The peacock with the most **eyespots** usually attracts the most females.

peacock feather

Male <u>birds of paradise</u> have brightly coloured feathers. They show them off by doing a special dance to attract females.

greater bird of paradise

There are more than 36 different types of birds of paradise.

You Can't See Me
– I'm Hunting!

Some animals, called **predators**, hunt other animals.

Some predators sneak up on their **prey**. They use their colouring to blend in with their surroundings, keeping them hidden.

The tiger's stripes look easy to see here ...

... but in long grass, the stripes make the tiger very hard to see.

The <u>Arctic fox</u> has a white coat that blends in with the snow.

You Can't See Me – I'm Hiding!

Some animals use colour to hide from predators. This helps keep them safe.

Can you spot this gecko?
Its skin is the same colour as the dead leaves.

This caterpillar uses its colour to blend into the leaf. It's almost invisible!

To Hide

To Hunt

Now You See Me...
Now You Don't!

Some animals can change their skin colour to match the background around them. This helps them hide from predators – and sneak up on their prey!

Cuttlefish change colour to hide from predators such as sharks. Cuttlefish often hunt crabs and small fish.

hiding

Flounder match their skin colour to the sea floor, where they hide from predators.

Flounder wait for shrimp or small fish to swim past – and then they eat them!

Eat a Colour!

Some animals change colour because of the food they eat.

Flamingos have grey feathers when they are born. Their feathers turn pink because of the foods they eat! These foods, such as shrimp and some seaweed, contain a special dye.

adult flamingo

baby flamingo

adult scarlet ibis

baby scarlet ibis

The scarlet ibis is brown when it is young. As it grows, its feathers turn bright red. This happens because the ibis eats shellfish, which contain a red dye.

Watch Out!

Sometimes bright colours mean danger.

The poison dart frog is the size of a paper clip. But even though it's tiny, it doesn't hide from predators. Its bright colour is a warning – its skin is poisonous! If a predator eats the frog, the predator will die.

Poison dart frogs can be lots of different colours.

A <u>coral snake's</u> bright colours
may look beautiful, but they are
a warning. Watch out, predators!
The coral snake is poisonous.

To Hide

To Hunt

Colourful Coral

Coral reefs have very clear water. This makes it easy for animals to see and be seen.

In a <u>coral reef</u>, being colourful is the best way to blend in. Some animals are hiding so they can hunt. Others are hiding to stay safe. Some do both!

This coral reef is in the Red Sea,
off the coast of Egypt.

Crack the Code

Each of these plants or animals uses their colour for a special reason. Can you match the right code to each one? Look back through the book to see if you are right.

cuttlefish

adult scarlet ibis

tiger

flounder

flower

greater bird of paradise

coral reef

caterpillar

adult flamingo

poison dart frog

berries

Arctic fox

coral snake

gecko

peacock

To Hide

To Be Seen

Food I Eat

! To Warn Off!

To Hunt

Glossary

attract: to draw attention

coral reefs: ocean areas filled with coral, where lots of fish and other animals live

eyespots: the patterns on a peacock's feathers, which look a bit like eyes

pollen: a yellow powder that bees carry from flower to flower

predators: animals that hunt other animals

prey: an animal that is hunted by another animal

Index